Contents

"One today is worth two tomorrows"
Benjamin Franklin

Scrapbooking
Made Easy

Kirsten Butts

Author: Kirsten Butts
Photography: Malcolm Cross

Scrapbooking Made Easy
Published in 2004 by Hinkler Books Pty Ltd
17–23 Redwood Drive
Dingley VIC 3172 Australia
www.hinklerbooks.com

ISBN 1-7412-1984-1
Printed and bound in China

What is Scrapbooking?

Scrapbooking *is the gathering together
and recording of precious memories, important events
and everyday happenings, using photos, memorabilia and journaling.
It is a way of preserving your family history in a way
that is both artistic and safe, so that it will be around for
future generations to enjoy.*

*Scrapbooking is getting those photos out of boxes and packets, sorting
through old newspaper clippings saved through the years
and gathering up those tickets to special events the family attended.
Then putting them into an album that is fun and beautiful
to look at, over and over again.*

*Most of all, scrapbooking is a way
to leave a part of you – a legacy.*

Why Scrapbooking?

Scrapbooking is one of the fastest growing hobbies today. This is because it's fun and creative – each scrapbook is as individual as the person who made it. However, the most important reason for scrapbooking is to get your photos into an acid and lignin-free environment, so they can be safely preserved for years to come.

Lignin is a substance present in wood fibre and pulp, and it is acidic. It is the acid in lignin that causes paper and photos to go brown and brittle, ruining our precious memories. Paper and paper products are considered acidic if their pH is lower than 7.0, which is acid-neutral (also known as alkaline).

"Archival", "acid-free" and "photo-safe" are all terms that describe paper, paper products and albums that have had the lignin removed and have a pH level above 7.0. These are considered safe to use with your precious photos.

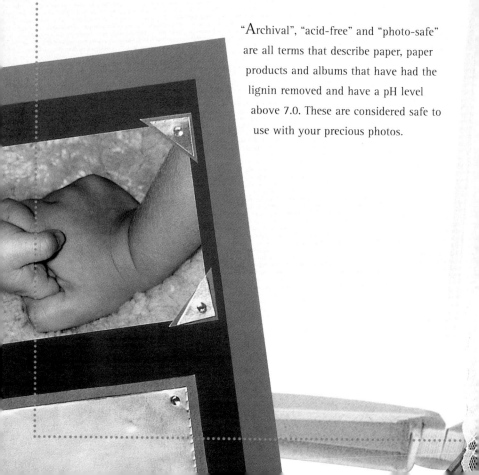

When scrapbooking, there will be times when you want to include things that aren't photo-safe, such as theater tickets, awards or newspaper clippings. Luckily, there are sprays you can use on these paper products that will neutralize the acid and make them safe to include.

For bulkier mementos you can use special memorabilia pockets and holders to keep the acid from affecting the rest of your scrapbook page. You can also get around this problem by taking color photocopies of mementos or scanning them onto acid-free paper.

"Happiness is a journey, not a destination."
Souza

How Do I Start?

It's easy to start scrapbooking! The first thing you need to do is get those photos in order. You might like to sort them chronologically, by people or by events. Whichever way you choose, find yourself a large clear space to work in. It will make the job easier if you have all your photos laid out in front of you.

When sorting your photos, have a separate pile for the ones you have difficulty placing. It's often easiest to sort these at the end, when you can look for things such as similar hair styles, clothes, cars etc.

Now go through your photos and say to yourself, "keep the best, get rid of the rest." Obviously you don't want to throw out that blurry, over-exposed photo if it's the only one you have of a particular person or occasion. But if it's one of many and you have other, better photos, then get rid of it. Remember, you'll still have the negative.

Where you go from here is entirely up to you. You can start working with your most recent photos and work your way back in time (your memories will be fresh, so you may find this easiest). You can start with the earliest photos and work chronologically (a year at a time). You can work by person (creating an album specifically for someone). Or you can work at random.

There is no right or wrong way to organize your photos, so decide what works best for you to keep you motivated, interested and excited.

"Do not the most moving moments of our lives find us without words?"
Marcel Marceau

What's On a Page?

:: title

:: background

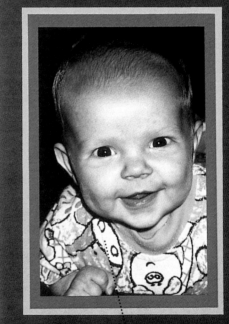

:: photos

:: *mat*

background ::
setting the mood

photos ::
the focal point of your page

mat ::
highlights your photos

title ::
names your page

journaling ::
documents memories and
recollections

embellishments ::
the 'icing on the cake'

:: *embellishments*

You are three months old.
You are smiling, laughing, and
cooing a lot. Still not sleeping or
eating very well, but with a face
like that you can get away with
anything.

:: *journaling*

Backgrounds

The backgrounds you choose for your page are very important. They will set the mood for your pages and may be subtle, bright, simple or busy.

Use the coloring or content of your photos as a guide for the background colors or patterns you choose. Think carefully about your photos – are they bright, happy baby photos? Perhaps they are wedding photos or snaps of a special holiday. Sometimes the right color will be obvious but at other times, you may have to think a little harder.

If you are having trouble deciding on a background, try placing your photos on several different background colors. This usually makes the choice much easier.

"A smile is the light in the window of your face, to show your heart is at home."

Unknown

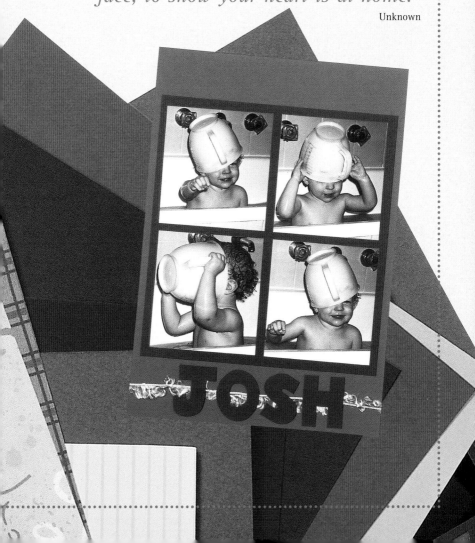

Photos

Your photos are the focal point of your page. After all, preserving them and your memories is the main reason you're scrapbooking!

Not every photo you choose to use on your page is perfectly framed and this is where cropping comes in handy. Cropping is trimming off the parts of a photo that detract from the main image – background that is distracting from the focus of your subject.

There are three things to remember when you are deciding whether or not to crop a photo:

1 :: Don't crop away part of the story. For example, sometimes the house, the car in the driveway or that pile of laundry sitting on the table behind your subject help to fill in the big picture. So take a second look before you crop.

2 :: Don't crop a photo that you don't have a negative for, such as a heritage photo. If you decide that you really need to crop a photo with no negative, it's best to make a copy and use that instead. Keep the original intact.

3 :: Don't cut into a Polaroid or instant photo.

"What you see depends on what you're looking for."
Unknown

There are no rules regarding how many photos you should or shouldn't put on a page. You don't have to use every single photo of an occasion on a page. Just choose the ones that tell the story. You can always store the rest of your photos in a photo-safe box or album to keep them safe. You may even use them on another page at a later date.

Mats

Mats are layers of card or paper that are different to the background of your page. They are placed behind your photos in order to frame, enhance and highlight them.

You can vary the look and style of your mats to suit the mood of your page and match the background color you have chosen. You can use a single (one layer), double (two layers) or even a triple (three layers) mat to frame your photo.

Mats can be narrow or wide.

Aunty Kathy sent this cozy over for you. You didn't fit into it by the time you went swimming, but I couldn't resist getting a photo. *Too cute.*

When creating a page, you don't have to mat all your photos in the same way. Try matting one main photo differently, to draw attention to it. Often this works best if you mat other photos on the page simply.

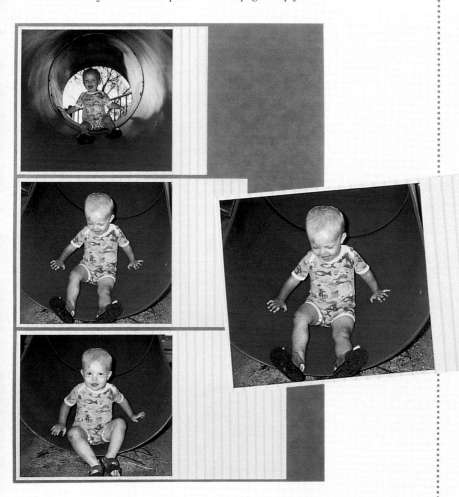

"*We don't stop playing because we grow old;
we grow old because we stop playing.*"

George Bernard Shaw

Titles

Titles are a quick way to give your pages personality.
They are as individual and varied as the pages you create.

A title can be situated anywhere on the page.

It can be a single word or an entire sentence.

It can be small or large.

It can state the obvious, or only have meaning for you.

Where'd you get that pencil grip

I hope you always stay friends

You can use your handwriting to create a title.

You can create a title on a computer.

Or you can use a template to create a title.

"Whether you think you can, or whether you think you can't, you're right!"

Henry Ford

Journaling

Journaling is an important part of scrapbooking – it is a written record to go with your treasured photos. It may be the story behind a particular photo or a heartfelt message to someone. It may be a list, recollections of a specific event, a letter, a quote, a song or a poem.

If you are unsure of where to start, then start with the facts!

Who's in the photo?

What's happening?

Where was the photo taken?

When was the photo taken?

Why is the photo important to you?

What do I feel when I look at this photo?

Make your journaling really count. Make it personal and genuine. Good journaling can bring a scrapbook page to life.

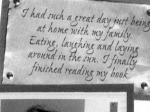

I had such a great day just being at home with my family. Eating, lunching and laying around in the sun. I finally finished reading my book.

Squishy squiggly wormy slippery slimy messy splashy wobbly

Alice and Sam

Talk Spaghetti 2001

When mum got the phone call to tell her she had won the holiday in Europe, she thought it was a hoax. But sure enough 6 months later she was flying out with Karen and Lynn for 3 weeks of unforgettable memories.

You can also ask yourself, "who am I writing this for?"
The answer to this question will change the "voice" you use when you are journaling.
If you write in the first person, you are recounting events that happened to you.
A message to your child might be written in the second person. For example,
"you liked this doll". Reporting details of an event that you are removed from
would be written in the third person (he, she, them).

Computers are becoming a huge part of scrapbooking and there are thousands of fonts to choose from, to add character to your journaling. However, don't forget that your handwriting is also a part of you. Make sure it is documented somewhere in your album.

Baby of Mine

Alice 3 months

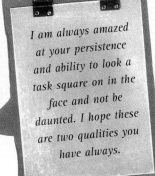

I am always amazed at your persistence and ability to look a task square on in the face and not be daunted. I hope these are two qualities you have always.

"A bird doesn't sing because
it has an answer, it sings
because it has something to say."

Maya Angelou

Embellishments

Embellishments are the decorations that you put on your page, to finish it off and give it that special look. They really are the icing on the cake!

Before you put anything on your page, ask yourself, 'is this safe for my photos?' If in doubt, make sure the embellishment is not directly in contact with any of your photos.

Mount it on acid-free paper or card, or place it in a memorabilia pocket or holder.

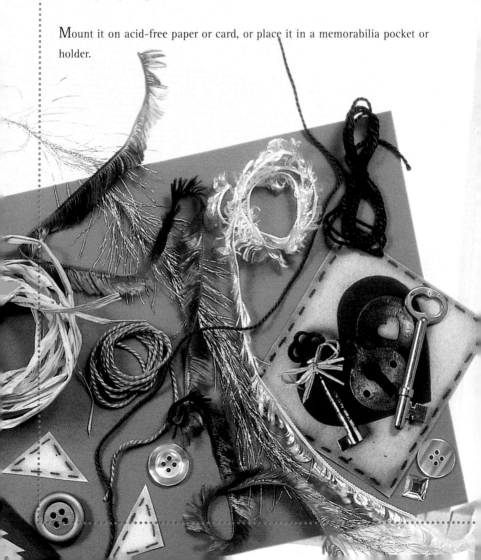

Your choice of embellishments is limited only by your imagination. Look at the theme of your page and try to come up with something really individual and exciting.

Be creative!

Joshua David 4th *December 2000* *4.45pm* *weight 4280g* *length 52.5cm*

"Be glad of life because it gives you a chance to love and to work and to play, and to look up at the stars."

Henry Van Dyke

Choosing a Color Scheme

Choosing a color scheme for your page can be confusing. Here is a very brief overview to help make your decision a little less daunting.

Primary colors are red, blue, and yellow.

Secondary colors are green, orange, and purple.
These are created when primary colors are mixed together.

Tertiary colors are yellow-green (lime), green-blue (turquoise), blue-purple (jacaranda), purple-red (magenta), red-orange (vermillion), and orange-yellow (pumpkin). These are created when primary and secondary colors are mixed together.

Neutral colors are black, white and grey.

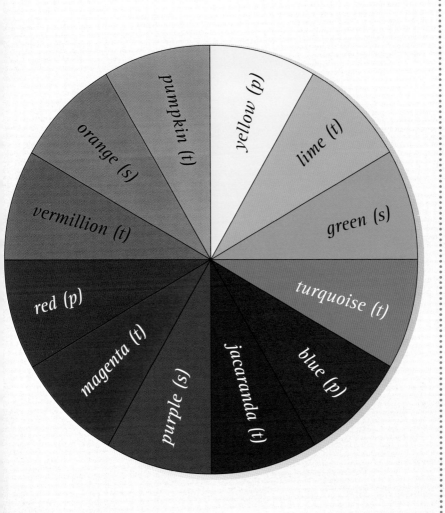

(p) ∷ *Primary colors*
(s) ∷ *Secondary colors*
(t) ∷ *Tertiary colors*

Choosing a Color Scheme (continued)

Now that you have the details of your color wheel, here are five ways to use it to give you a perfect color scheme every time!

1 :: Monochromatic – dark and light shades of the same color.

2 :: Analogous – three colors side by side.

3 :: Complementary – two colors opposite each other.

As soon as you woke up you wanted to open your presents

4 :: Contrasting – two colors separated by three spaces.

You took your time opening each present and having a good look at it before you opened the next one. You got the car you had been asking for, and duplo. You weren't very happy about me taking photos and told me to stop. You had a purple party at Nanny's house the following weekend with a jumping castle.

5 :: Triadic – three colors equally spaced.

Lastly, when deciding on the mood or theme for your page, remember that warm colors are yellow, orange, and red. Cool colors are blue, purple, and green. And you can use neutral colors anywhere.

"We are the music makers and we are the dreamers of the dream."

Arthur O'Shaunessey

Let's Get Started!

Now that you have all the basic information, let's make a page!

Start by choosing your photos – as few or as many as you want.

Crop the photos that need cropping, using a cutter which can be bought from a craft store. Place each photo on the photo cutting mat, position the edge of the ruler where you want to make the cut and then slide the cutting cartridge along, pressing down firmly. You will have more control if you are pulling the cartridge towards you. If you are feeling unsure, practise cutting some scrap paper first.

Lay the photos on the background paper you have chosen. Don't be afraid to move them around until you're happy with the placement. Remember to leave space for a title, journaling and embellishments.

Mat the photos. There are two ways you can do this. You can measure the photo and cut a mat to size, attaching the photo afterwards. Alternatively, you can attach the photo to the paper and then trim the desired width around the photo. Either way, the markings and measure-ments on your cutter and craft mat will take the guess work out.

Make the title and place it on the page. Remember, the size and style of the title is entirely up to you.

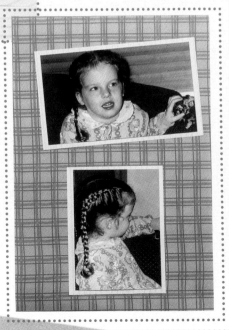

Let's get Started! (continued)

Now it's time to add the journaling to the page. You can write it directly onto the background paper, or you can write it on a separate, smaller piece of paper and attach it afterwards. Once again, how you add your journaling will depend on the theme and mood of your page, and the choice is entirely up to you.

You sat so still for such a long time and let me plait your hair for the first time. It's still one of my favorite ways to do your hair.

Choose some embellishments and place them around the photos, title and journaling. Move the embellishments around until you are completely happy that they are in the right places.

Once you are happy with the look of the page, you can stick everything down using acid-free adhesive.

Now stand back and admire your completed page. You have just

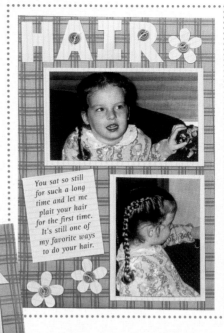

HAIR

You sat so still for such a long time and let me plait your hair for the first time. It's still one of my favorite ways to do your hair.

Plait **HAIR**

You sat so still for such a long time and let me plait your hair for the first time. Its still one of my favorite ways to do your hair.

created something unique that will remind you and your family of these times for years to come, whenever you look at it!

"Twenty years from now you will be more disappointed by the things you didn't do, than by the ones you did do. So throw off the bowlines. Sail away from the safe harbor. Catch the trade winds in your sail. Explore. Dream. Discover."

Mark Twain

Using an Alphabet Template

Templates are an inexpensive and versatile way to create titles and accents. They are a valuable addition to any scrapbooker's collection. Here's how to use an alphabet template:

Lay the template on the BACK of the paper you are using. Make sure that the template is actually BACK TO FRONT. This will ensure that the finished letter will be facing in the right direction. Tracing on the back of the paper also means you don't have to worry about erasing pencil lines, later.

Trace around the letters with a pencil.

Cut out the center parts of the letters you are using first. For example, the middle of the letters D, B or O.

Then use scissors to cut around the outside of the letters.

You may find that you need to use a sharp craft knife when you are cutting out smaller spaces, such as the middle of letters. Do this on your cutting mat to protect your work surfaces.

Using an Alphabet Template (continued)

Here are some simple ways to add interest to your basic letters, once you have cut them out:

Cut out the letters and glue them to a strip of contrasting colored paper.

Cut out the letters and glue them to individual squares of contrasting colored paper.

Cut the same letter out of solid color and patterned paper. Cut one letter in half horizontally and lay it over the top of the complete letter. Then glue them together.

Cut a letter from patterned paper, glue it to a piece of solid colored paper and then trim around it. This leaves an attractive border of solid colored paper around the letter.

Cut the same letter out of solid colored paper and patterned paper. Then lay the patterned paper letter on top but slightly higher and to the side. Glue the letters together so that the solid paper resembles a shadow.

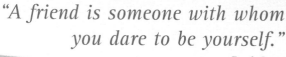

"A friend is someone with whom you dare to be yourself."

Frank Crane

Using a Shape Template

Shape templates are also a valuable addition to any scrapbooker's collection. They can be used to create fun and exciting embellishments, and help set the theme or mood of a page. Here's how to use the templates in your kit:

Place the shape template flat on the back of your chosen piece of paper.

Trace around the template with a pencil.

Cut the template out with some scissors (don't forget that you can use a sharp craft knife and your craft mat when cutting out small areas).

Glue the shape to your page for a fast, fun embellishment. You can also mix and match shapes for even more pizzazz!

Using the materials from the kit, cut a large heart from the patterned paper and a small heart from the solid colored paper. Then lay the small heart on top of the large heart and glue them together.

Cut a large flower from the solid colored paper and a large center circle from the patterned paper. Glue them together.

Now cut out some leaves and several more flowers and flower centers, both large and small. Bunch them together to form a bouquet.

Using a Shape Template (continued)

Cut a large tag from the solid colored paper and glue a small patterned heart to it. Or use a large heart and trim the edge.

Cut a large tag from the patterned paper and glue a large, solid colored leaf to it. Place the leaf on an angle for added effect.

Cut out a splat and use it as a background for letters, or a title.

Cut out two small tags, one patterned and one a solid color. Lay them over each other at an angle to make a heart shape and then glue them together.

Cut some shapes out and write your journaling on them, before sticking them to the page.

Use shapes as a photo mat, for a different look.

Cut out a large tag from solid colored paper. Then fold up the bottom of the tag and glue the sides. You now have a pocket!

Tearing

Tearing is a great way to add texture and interest to your scrapbook pages. It is also a quick way to create borders, backgrounds, photo mats and accents.

When tearing, you will have more control if you slowly tear towards your body, with one hand on either side, close to the tear. You will leave little creases on the paper if you are holding it too tightly, so a light grip is best.

Try practising tearing on scrap pieces of paper before you begin. Then you'll feel more confident when you come to tear that special piece of paper you're planning to use on your page.

2.8.99
David had some work to do
in Centennial park in the city
so we all went in.
After lunch we walked around
and played in the forest.

How fast and controlled you tear will determine how much of the "white core" of the paper you are working with is showing. There is no right or wrong amount; it is simply a matter of taste. The choice is yours.

As you become more experienced with tearing you will be able to create exactly the type of look you want, with different types of paper.

Tearing (continued)

For more control when tearing, try holding a ruler firmly on the paper and tearing against it. This will give a more regular finish to the tear.

You can also use a template to trace a shape or a letter onto your paper. Then, instead of cutting, simply tear the shape or letter out. This will give it a unique finish.

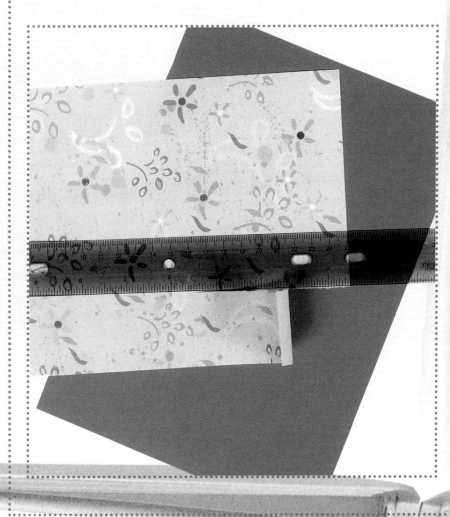

You can even crop your photos with tearing!

Use your imagination to create some unique effects with torn photos.

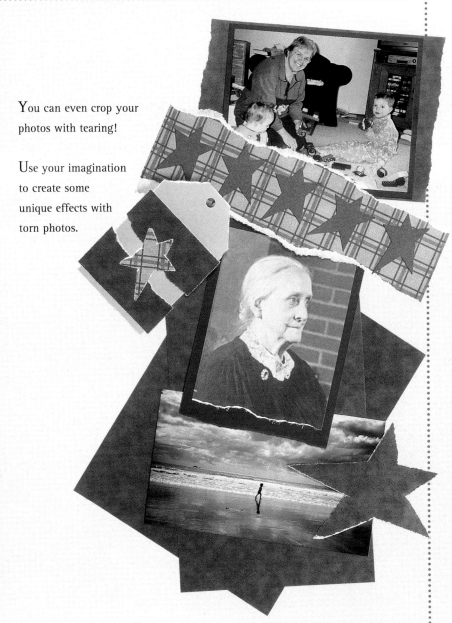

"Though we travel the world over to find the beautiful, we must carry it with us or we find it not."

Ralph Waldo Emerson

Buttons, String, Thread, and Ribbo

Now it's time to gather together all those old buttons and stray bits of string, thread and ribbon that you've stored in your sewing box. Just one of these can add old-world charm or country warmth to a page. If you don't happen to have a button or two lying around, or a length of beautiful ribbon, there are many styles, shapes and colors readily available.

You can simply glue string, thread, ribbons or buttons onto a page. Or you can actually sew them onto the paper with a needle and thread. If you are stitching onto a page, poke some guide holes in it with your needle first. This will act as a pattern and make it less likely that the paper will tear.

Use buttons as photo corners, mats or frames.

Stretch a piece of ribbon across the page and secure it with buttons for decoration. This is also a good way to secure photos, memorabilia or embellishments.

Create a fun hanger using buttons and thread.

Buttons, String, Thread and Ribbon

(continued)

Secure cut or torn shapes to the page with stitching. Poke a hole in the top of tag shapes and add some string or ribbon.

I know I haven't told you as much as I should .... I'm glad I married you!

Happy 9th Anniversary

Alice 6 months old You looked cute in dress Not a very practical thing for baby to wear, but it was fun every once in a while to dress you up ....

Cute as a ✿

Try using a button in a title, for an interesting effect.

Instead of cutting out the centers of your letters, stitch a button on.

Tie a bow and glue it to your page. Add a button for extra effect.

Use stitching with string or ribbon on your background paper.

"The best and most beautiful things in the world cannot be seen or even touched – they must be felt with the heart."

Helen Keller

Scrunching and Distressing

Scrunching and distressing are perfect ways to give your pages and embellishments an aged and worn look. They work especially well with tearing.

Take the piece of paper you wish to use and scrunch it into a ball.

Carefully straighten it back out and flatten it.

To flatten the paper out even more, you can iron it on a low heat if you wish.

To distress paper, you can use a kitchen scourer or a piece of very fine sandpaper.

Carefully rub the paper.

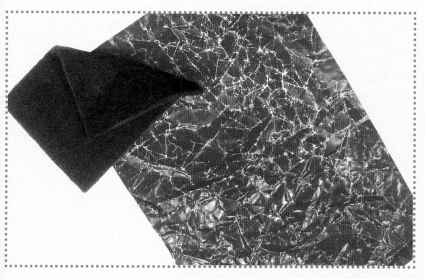

Pay special attention to the areas of the paper that would wear naturally under normal circumstances, such as edges and corners.

You may like to practise scrunching and distressing techniques on scrap paper first, to get the feel of using these techniques.

Scrunching and Distressing
(continued)

You can use scrunching and distressing techniques together, or on their own. The choice is yours and it all depends on what sort of effect you are creating on a page.

Try creating a page with a scrunched background.

A scrunched and distressed layout gives a dramatic effect.

Scrunched photo mats also look great.

Scrunched titles add a unique effect to a page.

Try creating a distressed title.

Scrunched shapes can make an interesting embellishment.

Distressed shapes also add interest to a page.

Add raffia or string to scrunching and distressing, for a great look.

Tearing, scrunching
and distressing
work well together.

No day at Darling
Harbor is complete
without a ride on
the merry go round.
It is enchanting.

"The supreme happiness in life is the
conviction that we are loved."

Victor Hugo

Cut-outs

Cut-outs are pre-made images and embellishments that you can mix and match to fit your page. They come in a wide range of themes and there is something available to suit just about every type of page.

You can simply cut them out and glue them to your page, or you can combine them with other embellishments and techniques to personalize them.

Like templates, cut-outs are a valuable addition to every scrapbooker's collection. You can keep a few handy, ready to use when you need that extra something for a special page.

Cut-outs work well with stitching.

Buttons and cut-outs often look great together, too.

Try including cut-outs, buttons and ribbons together on a page,
for a country look.

Cut-outs (continued)

Cut-outs and tearing give added texture to a page.

Cut-outs and shapes can complement each other.

Use cut-outs and a letter template to create unique titles.

You couldn't believe your luck when we didn't stop you from sticking your fingers in your cake. I think it was your favorite part of the day!
1st Birthday 4.12.2002

Joshua

Happy Birthday

Place string or raffia around cut-outs to give a natural look to your page.

You can even use cut-outs to add just the right touch to distressed or scrunched pages and mats.

"One of the advantages of being disorderly is that one is constantly making exciting discoveries."

A. A. Milne

Paper Piecing

Paper piecing is cutting pieces of paper or card into specific shapes and putting them together to create pictures. You can use a pre-made pattern, coloring book pictures, or you can create your own. You could also try tracing pictures. All you need is a simple line drawing.

You can use a photocopier or scanner to reduce or enlarge pictures if they aren't the right size.

Tooth Fairy

You figured out quickly that the tooth fairy brings you something when you lose a tooth! But instead of money you ask her for a toy.... what a generous tooth fairy.

Bear Hugs Sc

January 2002

Cut apart the separate pieces of the pattern.

Trace around the pieces with a pencil, onto the back of some paper.

Cut the pieces out, turn them over and glue them back together.

Once the paper pieces are together, you can use an acid-free marker to add some detail. A border or outline, a face or some stitching lines are often the perfect finishing touch.

Paper Piecing (continued)

The more you practise paper piecing and the more confident you become, the more complex your patterns can be.

Here are some patterns to get you started:

"If the only prayer you ever say in your life is thank you, it will be enough."

Meister Eckart

Weaving

Weaving is a great way to use up those leftover pieces of paper. You can weave an entire background, a photo mat, or simply use this technique to create one area of interest on a page.

Cut ten 1 centimeter (0.4 inch) strips of solid colored paper and ten 1 centimeter (0.4 inch) strips of patterned paper.

Lay the solid strips flat, side by side.

Take one piece of patterned paper and weave it through. Then continue with the remaining patterned strips.

Once you have finished, glue the ends together with acid-free glue.

You can make a loose or a tight weave.

You can also cut shapes from your woven paper.

You love the water! You were a little wary of the shower until Daddy held you.

Alice 6months

Water BABY

Mothers couldn't be everywhere so God created Aunties.
July 1999

"The heart has its reason, of which reason knows nothing."

Blaise Pascal

Conclusion

Now that you have begun making scrapbook layouts (pages), you should look at buying an album with page protectors to keep them safe.

There are several different sizes and styles of albums, so take the time to check out your options and find the album that suits you best. Your local scrapbooking store will be able to advise you and help you make this decision.

It's also a good idea to try and get together with other people in your area who are working on scrapbooks. Swapping ideas, stories and information are great ways to keep motivated and excited. Again, your local scrapbooking store will be able to help you with this.

Relax, have fun and happy scrapbooking!

Zoo Visit

The Giraffes are our favorite. The kids were entranced.

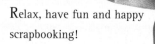

"Be silly. Be honest. Be kind."
Ralph Waldo Emerson

Glossary

Acid : : : : : : : : : : : a product used in paper manufacturing that is responsible for speeding up the deterioration of photos, turning them brown and brittle

Acid-free : : : : : : : refers to paper and products that have had the acid removed, therefore having a safe pH level

Alkaline : : : : : : : : pH levels above 7.0

Archival : : : : : : : : a term used to describe paper and products that have a pH level of 7.0 or above

Chalking : : : : : : : : a technique used to highlight and shade scrapbook pages using acid-free chalk or pastels

Circle cutter : : : : : a tool that will cut a perfect circle

Corrugated : : : : : : rippled or ridged paper or card

Crop : : : : : : : : : : : getting together with others to scrap and socialise

Cropping : : : : : : : : trimming your photos and paper

Card stock : : : : : : : heavier paper

Decorative scissors : : scissors that cut a pattern

Die-cut : : : : : : : : : a shape cut from paper or card using a die-cut machine

Dry embossing : : : : using a stylus to outline a pattern, shape or word on the back of paper or card, leaving a raised image on the front

Fonts : : : : : : : : : : : computer generated letters / alphabets

Journaling : : : : : : : documenting the who, what, where, when, and why of events on your scrapbook pages

Glossary (continued)

Layout :::::::::: another name for a scrapbook page

Lignin :::::::::: a substance naturally found in wood, and therefore in paper and paper products – lignin is acidic and unsafe for photo preservation

Memorabilia ::::: any mementos you have saved that hold special meaning for you

Memory book ::: another name for a scrapbook

Page protectors ::: acid-free polypropylene covers that slip over finished pages in a scrapbook

Personal trimmer :: a small, portable cutter

Photo safe ::::::: another term used to describe paper and paper products that have a safe acid level for use in scrapbooks

Punches :::::::: tools that cut shapes – there are many styles and sizes

Punch art ::::::: using punched shapes to create pictures

Red eye pen ::::: a special pen used to reduce the red eye effect in photos

Scraplift :::::::: to copy another layout (page)

Stickers :::::::: acid-free embellishments for scrapbook pages

Vellum :::::::::: plain or patterned transparent paper, often used in scrapping